“My Shorts R Bunching. Thoughts?”

Recent Books by G. B. Trudeau

Got War?

Talk to the Hand!

Dude: The Big Book of Zonker

Heckuva Job, Bushie!

Welcome to the Nerd Farm!

Tee Time in Berzerkistan

The Long Road Home: One Step at a Time
Foreword by Senator John McCain

The War Within: One More Step at a Time
Foreword by General Richard B. Myers

Doonesbury.com's The Sandbox:
Dispatches from Troops in Iraq and Afghanistan

Doonesbury.com's The War in Quotes

"My Shorts R Bunching. Thoughts?"

THE TWEETS OF ROLAND HEDLEY

By G. B. Trudeau

Andrews McMeel
Publishing, LLC

Kansas City • Sydney • London

DOONESBURY is distributed internationally by Universal Press Syndicate.

Some of the tweets in this book originally appeared in "Tweeps: The Tweets of Roland Hedley," *The New Yorker*, April 20, 2009.

09 10 11 12 13 RR2 10 9 8 7 6 5 4 3 2 1

ISBN-13: 978-0-7407-9109-3
ISBN-10: 0-7407-9109-5

Library of Congress Control Number: 2009930135

www.andrewsmcmeel.com

DOONESBURY may be viewed on the Internet at:
www.doonesbury.com and www.GoComics.com

"The creation of Twitter is as significant
and paradigm-shifting as the invention
of Morse code, the telephone, radio,
television, or the personal computer."

—Ashton Kutcher

Acknowledgments

After my tweet coverage of Obama's trip to the G-20 Summit was published in *The New Yorker* last spring, a great clamor arose for a more comprehensive collection of my work on the Twitter. A book seemed advisable, indeed unavoidable, given the terms of my latest divorce settlement, so I should begin these acknowledgments by noting how deeply indebted I am to my second wife.

I would also like to thank my longtime tweet feed producer, Lyn, but since she is always one wisecrack away from being sent back to Hooters, where I discovered her, I feel I must decline. She played no meaningful role in the successful completion of this project, indeed, impeded it with her frosty demeanor toward the author while steadfastly maintaining a mocking availability to co-workers other than him.

The author would also like to withhold appreciation from his producers at Fox News, without whose help this book was still possible—and very likely improved. Their contributions to every aspect of this endeavor—from researching to reporting to copyediting—were negligible. And because Rupert Murdoch, my boss of bosses, had smaller fish to fry, he, too, joins the ranks of those I need not thank.

Finally, no list of acknowledgments would be complete without shout-outs to White House colleagues Jake Tapper, Terry Moran, and Ed Henry, so regrettably, this list must remain incomplete. As they were of no assistance whatsoever, the author is most grateful not to be in their debt.

Roland Hedley
Washington, D.C.
August 9, 2009

Roland_Hedley

✔Following

My shorts are bunching. Thoughts?

10:15 AM Mar 4th from web

Checking out some hilarious graffiti in men's room at work. Will have production assistant transcribe.

10:18 AM Mar 4th from TwitterBerry

My chest mole, kissed by princesses and "it" girls, looks infected. May swing by dermatologist after lunch.

7:46 AM Mar 5th from web

Interviewing new mistress after the broadcast tonight. Send me your questions.

8:04 PM Mar 5th from txt

Online auction of Gandhi memorabilia. Bid on sandals but no luck. Was going to bronze and give to nephew, peacenik back in day.

2:45 PM Mar 6th from txt

Asked by Columbia Journalism Review for comment on Rupert Murdoch. Refused to go on record calling him a dick.

8:51 PM Mar 6th from web

You'll never guess who I'm sitting in the Nightline green room with, because I certainly have no idea. He looks sketchy, like TARP guy.

9:11 PM Mar 6th from TwitterGadget

Holding three of a kind, Nightline booker down to her Danskins, 12 minutes to air. Do I go all-in?

10:18 PM Mar 6th from TwitterGadget

Off to buy big-ass flat-screen for bathroom. Have a $400 credit at Circuit City. Helping the economy, yo. Taking houseboy to schlep.

9:00 AM Mar 7th from web

BTW, FYI, I may have to let my houseboy go soon. Just wanted to give you heads-up, because I know some of you were close to Ding.

9:02 AM Mar 7th from web

It's night. Bathed in LED light from a dozen winking devices, I toss, turn. What are you hiding, Tim Geithner? Open the kimono, baby!

12:05 AM Mar 8th from web

Roland_Hedley

✔Following

From '95: What's the difference between Rush and the Hindenburg? One's a flaming Nazi gasbag, other's just a dirigible. Still true? Discuss.

9:39 AM Mar 8th from twhirl

Been working on my blog. Just posted an item reporting that I was about to tweet. Really good comments so far.

1:02 PM Mar 8th from web

Been wading through Times. What Rick Sanchez tweeted about print giving him a headache is so true. Can't wait for newspapers to be over.

5:30 PM Mar 8th from web

Just withdrew lunch with me from online charity auction. Bidders failed to meet minimum $5K bid. People are really hurting out there.

11:51 AM Mar 10th from web

Another tanning booth mishap, this time with squirrely field unit. Will need remedial makeup for show. How does Brian Williams do it?

12:03 PM Mar 10th from TwitterBerry

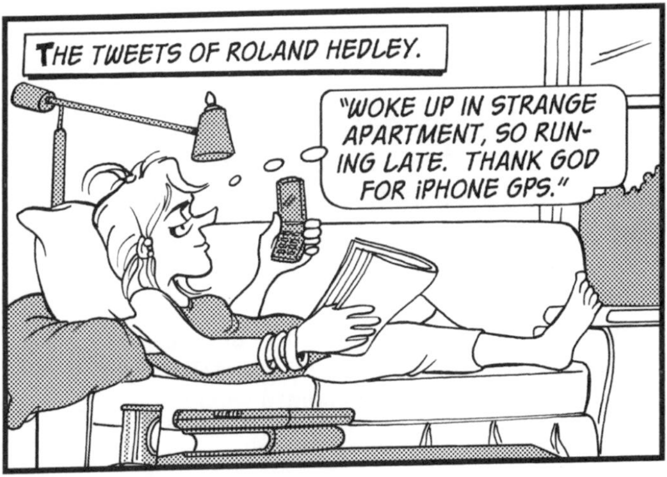

THE TWEETS OF ROLAND HEDLEY.
"WOKE UP IN STRANGE APARTMENT, SO RUNNING LATE. THANK GOD FOR iPHONE GPS."

When I look back on today, I know I'll cherish the memory of Rick Sanchez's 13 tweets and Chris Cuomo's 22 tweets. And it's only 3:20 p.m.

3:24 PM Mar 13th from web

Update 4:37 p.m., EST: When I look back on today, I know I'll cherish the memory of Rick Sanchez's 103 tweets and Chris Cuomo's 172 tweets.

4:37 PM Mar 13th from web

GMA's Cuomo finishes day w/ 232 tweets. Like the rest of us aren't even here. Remember "Hustler" scene where Newman gets his thumbs broken? Just askin'.

11:33 PM Mar 13th from web

Roland_Hedley

✓Following

Stand by for my next tweet. Will be pulling no punches. Please retweet this alert to your followers so they can stand by as well.

1:39 PM Mar 14th from Twitterrific

Sorry, stand down. My feed producer dropped the ball on this tweet, but blaming intern. POTUS right about no one taking responsibility anymore.

2:45 PM Mar 14th from Twitterrific

Another hissy fit from my tweet feed producer, who seems to have forgotten I discovered her at Hooters. Who busts stones in THIS economy?

5:14 PM Mar 14th from Twitterrific

Just took Ambien. Long day, blogger's block but answered 179 tweets, no time to unwind, 5 a.m. call but still racing. Might take Ambien.

12:17 AM Mar 15th from web

Whoa. What time is it?

11:53 AM Mar 15th from web

Just caused fender bender on Beltway by tweeting on my way to work. Lesson learned.

9:12 AM Mar 16th from TwitterBerry

Just had another fender bender. Thanks to followers who responded to first accident. Feeling your relief that I'm OK.

9:39 AM Mar 16th from TwitterBerry

NY AG demanding names of AIG bonus execs. Let's make 'em famous, gang. See to it that within 24 hours, their children are taunted at school.

4:22 PM Mar 16th from web

Disregard that last tweet from a staffer.

4:24 PM Mar 16th from web

Have now dated 2 Ana Marie Cox impostors in a row. Anyone got hard AMC 411 (last 4 SS# digits, identifying marks) so don't get burned again?

6:17 PM Mar 16th from web

I hate America. There, I just said in 15 characters what Frank Rich needed 9,982 characters to say in his column today.

11:57 PM Mar 18th from web

OMIGOD — DAVID GREG-ORY JUST ATE A HAM SANDWICH!
WOW... SAYS WHO?
HE JUST TWITTERED HIS FAN BASE. I FOLLOW THE TWEETS OF ALL MY FAVE NEWS PERSONALITIES!
AS A FOLLOWER, YOU NOT ONLY LEARN WHAT'S HAP-PENING NOW, YOU SOME-TIMES GET A HEADS-UP ON WHAT'S **ABOUT** TO HAPPEN!
"ABOUT TO SCRATCH MYSELF, STAND BY."
BIP! BIP! BIP!

Roland_Hedley

✓Following

Should all of us at Fox News say "Democrat Party" the way Newt & Rush still do? I'm worried that Dems will start saying "Repube Party." Thoughts?

7:16 AM Mar 19th from txt

When I was a kid, used to go door to door telling people the news. At end of month, would collect micropayments. Biz model for Twitter?

10:09 AM Mar 20th from web

All over town, players claiming they "get it." Big whoop. I not only get it, but bring it—and put it in every tweet, yo.

3:37 PM Mar 20th from web

Sorry, have at least three shovel-ready, in-depth tweets I'd like to report and feed, but can't get green-lit by net. Must be the economy.

8:58 PM Mar 21st from web

Staff is pruning follower list. Need to deliver quality demo to potential feed sponsors, so if you're reading this, you made the cut. Props.

9:48 PM Mar 22nd from Winbox

Roland_Hedley

✓ Following

At AIG hearing, hottest ticket in town, doing color tweets. All the top Twitterers here, very competitive environment. Wish me luck!

9:49 AM Mar 18th from Tweetie

Placeholder tweet. Lot of sharp elbows here fighting for tweetspace. My advice? Stay with a microblog brand you trust as much as this one.

9:59 AM Mar 18th from Tweetie

No tweeting allowed in hearing room, so keep bending over to "tie shoelaces" to conceal tweeting. Guard suspicious. I'm at great risk.

10:31 AM Mar 18th from Tweetie

Just spotted colleague Terry Moran in hall. Could wave, but easier to tweet. Hey, dude.

10:49 AM Mar 18th from Tweetie

AIG honcho Ed Liddy still no-show. Probably vomiting in the men's room. Gonna go check. Be right back.

10:50 AM Mar 18th from Tweetie

"LET'S NOT THROW STONES AT AIG BONUS HOLDOUT GUY. MAY HAVE HAD HIS REA- SONS. FOR INSTANCE, WHO AMONG US HAS NEVER HAD A SERIOUS COKE PROBLEM?"

Saw Geithner after presser, confronted him about bonuses, toxic assets, his tax problems, etc. Unfortunately he was out of screaming range.

1:08 PM Mar 23rd from web

Followed up with a scorching private tweet. No reply yet.

1:09 PM Mar 23rd from web

Market up again. Park Avenue got K Street to push Pennsylvania Avenue to go Madison Avenue to sell Wall Street to Main Street? So wrong.

3:55 PM Mar 26th from TwitterFox

ROLAND, ARE NON-STOP TWEETS REALLY THE BEST USE OF YOUR TIME?
JUST TRYING TO STAY COMPETITIVE, ED.
BIP! BEEP! BIP!
ALL THE OTHER BIG DOGS ARE MICRO-BLOGGING THEIR FANS. NO **WAY** I'M CEDING THE LOW GROUND TO YOUR RICK SANCHEZES OR DAVID SHUSTERS!
BESIDES, WHEN YOU GET DOWN TO IT, WHICH WOULD YOU RATHER HEAR ABOUT — SOME DEPRESSING NEWS ON THE ECONOMY OR WHAT ISLAND I PICKED FOR MY VACATION?
©B Trudeau
PLEASE LET THAT BE A REAL QUESTION.
OF COURSE IT IS — I'M A JOURNALIST!
BIP! BIP! BIP!

Roland_Hedley

✓Following

At Dulles, on way to London for G-20 summit. In taxi to airport, practiced my English accent on Irish cab driver, which didn't go well.

3:15 PM Mar 30th from TwitterGadget

En route UK. Just re-upped membership in 1st class Mile High Club. Okay, by myself, but was thinking of flight attendant.

10:45 PM Mar 30th from TweetDeck

Disregard that last tweet from a staffer.

10:47 PM Mar 30th from TweetDeck

How bad is UK economy? My tailor is personally picking me up at Heathrow. Will post twitpix of swatches en route hotel for your input.

11:14 PM Mar 30th from web

Idea for iPhone app: You launch it and YOUR GODDAMN PLANE DOESN'T SUDDENLY DROP 3,000 FT TO AVOID MID-AIR COLLISION! I'd pay $1.99 for that.

5:31 AM Mar 31st from web

Roland_Hedley

✓Following

This is Lyn Swit, Roland's tweet producer, pre-positioned in UK. Will be covering RBH's arrival in London.

8:36 AM Mar 31st from TwitterFox

Lyn again. RBH's plane diverted to Reykjavik. Reports: "Icelandic women heart-stoppingly hot. Downside: They're all living in their cars."

10:39 AM Mar 31st from TwitterFox

London. City bracing for demos. Bankers told to come to work in jeans. Which means they'll look like the anarchists. What's wrong with that plan?

1:03 PM Mar 31st from web

Went to use Bank of England ATM to test solvency, received ten sterling notes and head wound. Now @ Chelsea ER, testing socialized medicine.

2:23 PM Apr 1st from web

At ER, watching ER chat up POTUS on telly. Mrs. POTUS blocking camera lights, her shadow plunging tiny queen into darkness. Human eclipse.

2:51 PM Apr 1st from web

No one here will accept payment for my sutures. I feel like I'm in a Cuban clinic, only without the humidity and livestock.

3:18 PM Apr 1st from web

FLOTUS grazes Queen's arm, violating inane, 600-year-old protocol.

3:19 PM Apr 1st from twhirl

Theory why protocol exists: Nobody ever WANTED to touch queen, starting with Liz I, owing to thick, white makeup and cold fish factor.

9:13 AM Apr 2nd from web

Think I'll stir the pot and report previous tweet as fact. We report, you decide.

9:14 AM Apr 2nd from web

Breaking. Historically, nobody ever wanted to touch the queen due to unattractiveness. To avoid embarrassment, protocol was created.

9:17 AM Apr 2nd from web

Just for the record, in my storied career, I have touched 16 heads of state, all above the waist, and only been detained once.

6:03 PM Apr 2nd from web

Roland_Hedley

✔Following

Handling pool tweets on Air Force One to Strasbourg in a.m. Need to steal something cool from plane for kids. Suggestions?

10:23 PM Apr 2nd from Winbox

BO appeared in press cabin. Your pool reporter was ready with tuff Q's, but POTUS hit him with high beams and he went stupid. Next time.

7:20 AM Apr 3rd from Winbox

Stole fire extinguisher from Air Force One. No WH logo, but I need one for my boat.

7:22 AM Apr 3rd from Winbox

Sarkozy says he's willing to take a Gitmo prisoner. Wonder if Madonna would take one. Her people should check it out.

10:53 AM Apr 3rd from web

Carla/FLOTUS couture catfight reminds me of my own fashion face-offs w/ Peter Jennings back in the day. How the cashmere flew!

3:28 PM Apr 3rd from web

Carla v. FLOTUS? C'mon. One of them Harvard Law, the other slept w/ Donald Trump. No contest. Trump's huge, even here.

6:16 PM Apr 3rd from web

Proposal: World media mock N. Korea missile dud 24/7. Shamed Dear Leader shoots top scientists, crippling program for yrs. Flaws?

10:19 AM Apr 4th from web

Foreign reporters cheered POTUS after presser. No one even threw shoe, for balance. International community has such a liberal bias.

2:20 PM Apr 4th from txt

Roland_Hedley

✔ Following

Okay, so POTUS was BaRock Star Da Bomba at Summit presser. I know, I work for the other side, but he so was.

4:41 PM Apr 4th from web

Watching Bush, thought: I could do better. Watching BHO, think: He's not one of us. From another galaxy. Digging into it.

5:10 PM Apr 4th from web

Here's what I've got so far: Father was in fact an alien. Mother grew up in what's being described as "fly-over country."

5:24 PM Apr 4th from web

What does he want? Does he come in peace? Or is nationalization prelude to colonization? Thoughts?

5:25 PM Apr 4th from web

Planning trick question for next presser: "How many parsecs is it from the Pleiades to Omega Nebula?" If he knows, nailed!

5:34 PM Apr 4th from web

Ankara. Bought a chunk of hash for my oldest. Everyone on press bus went ape-shit. What the heck is "Midnight Express"?

11:16 PM Apr 5th from TweetDeck

Oh, that "Midnight Express."

11:18 PM Apr 5th from TweetDeck

Okay, ditched hash, planted it on Le Monde reporter. Thanks for caring, Tweeps, never gotten 180 direct messages before.

11:22 PM Apr 5th from TweetDeck

Miss quality time with kids. Quantity time not so much, cuz I can be pretty busy on Saturdays, when I get them.

4:07 PM Apr 6th from txt

I get Blago doing Disney just before indictment. I went to Sea World the day my Jag was repossessed. Times like that, you want to be in a happy place.

9:04 PM Apr 6th from web

BTW, my kids wild about Disney World. Sked too crazy to take them, but I love reading the brochures to them at bedtime.

9:07 PM Apr 6th from web

ED, I'M NOT SURE YOU UNDERSTAND WHAT MY TWEETS MEAN TO MY FOLLOWERS...
WHEN I TWITTER, IT HUMANIZES ME – IT BRINGS ME DOWN OFF MT. OLYMPUS!
MY FOLLOWERS GET A CHANCE TO SEE THE STAR BEHIND THE MYTH! AND THE FEEDBACK LOOP MAKES THEM FEEL LIKE STAKEHOLDERS IN A STORIED CAREER!
SORRY. I HAD NO IDEA.
"MY SHORTS ARE BUNCHING UP. THOUGHTS?"
BIP!
BIP!
BIP!
BEEP!

Home! Thanks for following, everyone. Great thing about Twitter—all the gratification of being big enough to attract stalkers, none of the danger.

1:30 PM Apr 7th from web

En route DC to Baghdad to cover POTUS departure home. Thanks for the 12,000 mile head-fake, Gibbs.

2:02 PM Apr 7th from twhirl

Descent into Baghdad corkscrew death-spiral thru blinding sandstorm. Same vibe as 2nd marriage. Tell ex thinking of her.

3:25 PM Apr 7th from twhirl

@ Camp Victory w/ FLOTUS. Michelle rocking body armor, but no fashion face-off w/ Mrs. Maliki, who may not even exist.

3:58 PM Apr 7th from web

FLOTUS rips off Kevlar to show bare arms to 30 startled Iraqi schoolgirls bused in from Syrian refugee camp.

4:01 PM Apr 7th from web

Chaperone looks aroused.

4:02 PM Apr 7th from web

Roland_Hedley

✓ Following

Flying on to Kabul. Won't be tricked by WH twice. Per Bush, "Fool me once, shame on you. Fool me twice, shame on you."

4:06 PM Apr 7th from txt

So not ONE of you could've warned me POTUS not going to Kabul, where I am now? What is point of Twitter, exactly?

10:47 AM Apr 8th from web

Kabul. Relaxing on Google Images. Sad commentary how many pix there are of Megan Fox, how few of Edward R. Murrow.

10:11 PM Apr 8th from web

Kabul. Awakened by huge blast in hotel lobby. Suicide bomber blew up complimentary breakfast buffet. Off to find bagel.

7:14 AM Apr 9th from web

Kabul. Looking for one honest man. Offered 37 bribes today, all accepted. May have to lower offer ($2) or switch to honest women.

10:57 AM Apr 9th from web

Feel like bribed half the city, people bowing to me as I drive by. Did you know that for 75¢, cop will let you park in a mosque?

1:32 PM Apr 9th from web

BTW, using body double for interviews. Fighting with NY to get one for producer but budget tight. Lyn SUCH a good sport.

8:24 PM Apr 9th from web

Producers never get credit they deserve. If I get Emmy for Kabul report, would want Lyn in audience so I could mention her.

8:57 PM Apr 9th from web

Lyn here, tweeting from inside burqa while Roland's body double interviews warlord. Would someone please contact embassy? Want to go home.

10:36 AM Apr 10th from Tweetie

Heading for airport. Anyone heard from Lyn?

10:42 PM Apr 10th from web

Midnight flight to Kandahar. No Lyn. Probably out clubbing. Tired of covering for her.

11:55 PM Apr 10th from Winbox

"TWINTERVIEWED JIHADIST AT KABUL KFC. COMMON GROUND: WE BOTH HATE THE YANKEES. DIFFERENCE: HE HATES ALL THE OTHER TEAMS, TOO."

Being driven in Humvee to air field by Army public affairs officer. Mesmerized watching her assets redeploy every time we hit bump.

3:14 PM Apr 11th from web

PAO briefing me on enemy activity. Trying not to yawn. She's too young to know how much action I saw BEFORE nanny fabrics like Kevlar.

3:27 PM Apr 11th from web

PAO fluent in Pashto, Dari, and Arabic. Overkill. I find Spanglish works most places. It's the Swiss Army knife of languages.

3:58 PM Apr 11th from web

Simone, my PAO, went to West Point. Lyn would be so jealous if . . . Oh, shit, Lyn! Anyone heard from her?

4:10 PM Apr 11th from web

Base under attack. Apparently routine. Will try to describe sound of incoming. PHOOMPH! Bracka-bracka! Eeeee . . . KaWHOOM!

11:01 PM Apr 11th from web

Brat-a-brat-brat!!! PHOMPH! PHOMPH! Buddah-buddah-buddah! BRAT! BRAT! THBOOM! Eeee . . . KaWHOOM! Shhhhzzzt!

11:03 PM Apr 11th from web

That last one was my pants ripping. Will explain later . . .

11:03 PM Apr 11th from web

Almost at . . . Buddah-buddah! WaFOOOOM! . . . bunker . . . Zip! zip! . . . please, God, let me . . . THRAKKADAADA!!! My pants!

11:13 PM Apr 11th from web

Pants okay. Retrieved under fire by Simone. New respect for her. From now on, will soak up her briefings like ShamWow.

11:40 PM Apr 11th from web

Roland_Hedley

✔Following

Getting complaints from tweeps who miss knowing what I'm eating. They have a Mickey D's on base, so today had a #4 with pie.

2:00 PM Apr 12th from web

Still no word from my producer Lyn. Weird. Will have to look her up when I get back home.

9:08 AM Apr 12th from web

Got fresh pants at PX. Old cargoes basically totaled, will donate to a local orphanage that gets cable, so kids will know me.

11:12 AM Apr 12th from web

Proud day for America off Somalian coast. While Captain Phillips pees off lifeboat, pirates left holding dicks.

4:25 PM Apr 12th from web

Sorry for the vulgar imagery of last tweet. Part of the rough culture of a NATO base.

5:30 PM Apr 12th from web

Another mortar attack. Can't move about, so at rec center watching "Mall Cop."

8:37 PM Apr 12th from web

To paraphrase colleague Geraldo, if you have children around, I implore you, BEG you, not to let them read my next tweet.

9:26 PM Apr 12th from web

Talibs breached wire last night. Base on lockdown. Going bowling.

8:24 AM Apr 13th from web

ABC News gets it wrong: Phillips tied up, not peeing, when SEALs took out pirates. @GStephanopoulos dead to me.

8:35 AM Apr 13th from web

While on Humvee patrol, used on-board computer to order Ab Rocket. And because I acted when I did, receiving second one absolutely free.

8:01 PM Apr 13th from web

Sorry, military's SERE training works. Took course @ Learning Annex years ago, have never once made false confession. Stop hating on freedom!

9:43 PM Apr 13th from web

ANOTHER TWEET FROM ROLAND HEDLEY!
WHAT NOW?
"QUOTE OF THE DAY: 'JESUS SAVES! BUT GRETZKY GETS THE RE-BOUND AND SCORES!'"
"FUNNY QUOTE, ROLAND! WHO SAID THAT?"
BIP! BIP! BIP!
"ANONYMOUS."
BIP! BIP! BIP!
©B Trudeau

Sorry can't cover upcoming POTUS speech, but won't apologize for being w/ our men/women in uniform. Will retweet WH colleagues to fill void.

10:21 AM Apr 14th from web

RT @davidgregory Having trouble following President's speech. Wish @Roland_Hedley had my back here.

10:53 AM Apr 14th from web

RT @jaketapper Gulp. POTUS speech way over my head. @Roland_Hedley, where are you?

10:56 AM Apr 14th from web

RT @katiecouric Working on Idol story in LA, missing Prez speech. Thank God for riveting retweets from @Roland_Hedley in Kandahar.

11:03 AM Apr 14th from web

RT @edhenrycnn POTUS obfuscating. Wish I could interrupt with tuff q's like @Roland_Hedley, who always brings it.

11:20 AM Apr 14th from web

RT @ricksanchezcnn Prez criticizing 24-hour news culchur. Are we rilly on air 24 hours? Seems like @Roland_Hedley is on 25 hours!

11:30 AM Apr 14th from web

Roland_Hedley

▶ ✔Following

Conductong ofg thw recprd intwrvoew w, Dutch comnandef of NatO basw. Tweetinf im pocket,,,

12:51 PM Apr 14th from UberTwitter

Dutch recklessly peaceful. There will never be a Netherlandian Century.

1:32 PM Apr 14th from UberTwitter

History nerds replying Dutch already had their own century. Tulip Bubble doesn't count.

1:38 PM Apr 14th from UberTwitter

Hosted Fox tea bagger @ PX, razzed for intellectual incoherence. Turns out we DO have representation. Thx for heads up, NY.

2:33 PM Apr 15th from web

Moved teabagger to local village. Wise-ass elder asked why I wasn't dressed as Native American.

4:52 PM Apr 15th from web

AP confirms full representation + biggest tax cut in history. Management shit-fit to come. Wouldn't want to be moron who suggested tea party motif.

11:13 PM Apr 15th from web

Popular Mechanics reporting tea bags invented in 1903. Analogy now in tatters.

4:18 PM Apr 16th from web

En route Helmand to meet w/ warlord. Most journalists not up to 3 days of rutted roads, IEDs, bandits, etc., so taking chopper.

4:48 PM Apr 16th from TwitterBerry

Greeted at Helmand LZ by Buz Kashi, local Pashtun boss. Tells me not to call him "warlord," prefers "druglord."

8:23 AM Apr 17th from web

Translator says Buz Kashi means "goat-puller." Don't ask. I did, and I regret it.

8:23 AM Apr 17th from web

Drug lord regular guy, does interview in kitchen near stack of laundry. Later, stack of laundry moves; it's his wife! LOL

11:57 AM Apr 17th from web

Roland_Hedley

✓ Following

Opium so cheap Buz hands me large brick as gift. Decline, knowing Air India charges for extra weight. Also, illegal, wrong.

4:55 PM Apr 17th from web

Meet with Marja poppy farmer. Explains his poppies grown for flower arrangements at Thai weddings. Tired of being lumped in.

10:05 AM Apr 18th from web

Suggest poppy farmer grow chia instead, export seeds for Chia Pets. Blank stare. These people don't want to be helped.

10:06 AM Apr 18th from web

Tell farmer about my Samuel L. Jackson Chia Pet. Fond memories of little green Afro in kitchen window. Rat on, rat on!

10:07 AM Apr 18th from web

Tense meeting between tribal types and US Army captain in local opium storage shed. I am fly on wall, one of about 30,000.

10:22 AM Apr 19th from web

Nervous US officer makes offer. Wizened elder spits, tosses headless mongoose carcass on table. This can't be good.

10:27 AM Apr 19th from web

False alarm. Mongoose is lunch. Whew.

10:31 AM Apr 19th from web

Comical stalemate over who should eat first. Meanwhile, 30,000 flies living large.

10:35 AM Apr 19th from web

Roland_Hedley

✔Following

Captain eats Lord of Flies entrée, asks if traditional dish. Elder laffs, sez got idea from "Survivor." Captain goes outside to call in air strike.

10:30 AM Apr 19th from web

Overheard: "Request strafe, stand by for cords, over." "Tango 3, say sit-rep, over." "Nearly poisoned, over." "Dude, get a grip. Out."

11:01 AM Apr 19th from web

Tempers cool, confab reboots. Mongoose removed, contrite warlords send out for Chinese. Captain regains face, orders school built.

2:34 PM Apr 19th from web

Tuff negotiations. Pashtuns offer to stop glaring at U.S. patrols, Captain offers to not drop bombs on new school.

2:36 PM Apr 19th from web

Talks stall. I suggest warlords host Pashtun Poppy Parade, putting Talibs to work on floats, giving them stake in new Afghanistan.

2:38 PM Apr 19th from web

Captain asks me to leave. I have to pee anyway.

2:39 PM Apr 21st from web

Unzipping in poppy field, think about Dorothy, teaching generation to view opium as sleep aid. How can Hollywood sleep at night?

2:45 PM Apr 21st from web

Returning Kabul in Army Blackhawk to reset and prepare for tweet death-match w/ archrival @AnnCurry.

6:56 PM Apr 22nd from TwitterFox

Flying into Kabul, wondering what I used to do with the two hours a day I now spend on Twitter. Probably just wasted them.

7:11 PM Apr 22nd from TwitterFox

In response to previous tweet, several followers offer intervention when I return. One of them has a hot avatar, so made appointment.

9:35 AM Apr 23rd from TwitterFox

Starting day by re-reading @SamChampion real-time tweets on having skin growth removed. Reminds me why I'm a journalist.

9:04 AM Apr 24th from web

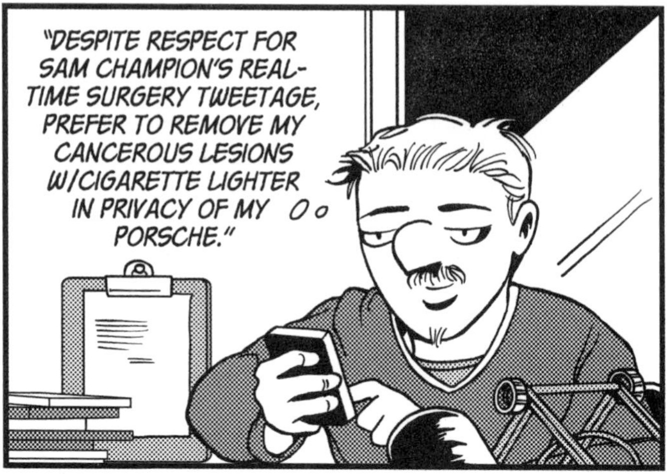

"DESPITE RESPECT FOR SAM CHAMPION'S REAL-TIME SURGERY TWEETAGE, PREFER TO REMOVE MY CANCEROUS LESIONS W/CIGARETTE LIGHTER IN PRIVACY OF MY PORSCHE."

No good stories breaking in failed narco-state, so @ Kabul Intercontinental Hotel pool enjoying well-deserved me day.

9:59 AM Apr 24th from Twitterrific

Correction, per Fox News stylebook. Stand by for revised tweet.

10:00 AM Apr 24th from Twitterrific

No good stories breaking in fledgling democracy, so @ Kabul Intercontinental Hotel pool enjoying well-deserved me day.

10:01 AM Apr 24th from Twitterrific

Nemesis @AnnCurry stands down, flees Kabul. Final count for tweet death-match, 12-7 moi. And I didn't do cooking tweets.

11:24 AM Apr 26th from web

Need bigger story than fledgling democracy. En route Islamabad to watch city fall as 500,000 troops guard Indian border.

11:25 AM Apr 26th from TwitterBerry

How bad is it? 30 miles north of Islamabad, it's now illegal to shave, fly a kite, or be a girl. That's how bad.

11:26 AM Apr 26th from TwitterBerry

Want to get to capital before formal handover of missile launch codes to illiterate psycho-jihadists. Could be historic.

11:26 AM Apr 26th from TwitterBerry

Will try to Twitpic photo of madrasa grads holding football. No promises.

11:27 AM Apr 26th from TwitterBerry

Mood here reminds me of fall of Saigon, when I had less than 20 minutes to close down Time magazine sports desk (I overslept).

8:54 AM Apr 27th from TwitterBerry

Roland_Hedley

✓Following

Woke up today w/ fever, chills, lack of appetite, fatigue, vomiting, and diarrhea. Must be the jet lag.

9:21 AM Apr 27th from web

Now sweating profusely. Might find a movie theater to cool off.

9:22 AM Apr 27th from web

After wild coughing fit, settled in to watch witless Bollywood film. Only final dance number was believable. Left me giddy, dizzy, nauseous.

10:45 AM Apr 27th from web

City in lockdown. Adjusted number of checkpoints seen by this reporter: 68. Actual number: 136 (owing to double vision).

11:38 AM Apr 27th from web

This is Islamabad Police Officer A. Razi. The owner of this device asked me to type, "It's all good." It's not, but th

2:22 PM Apr 27th from web

Lyn here, finally caught up w/ RH, in hospital with regular (not swine) flu. Apparently he panicked, drank bottle of hand sanitizer.

5:56 PM Apr 27th from Tweetie

Lyn here. Roland says thanks for get-well tweets from all of you except @Fake_Jesus and @Oprah, who are dead to him. They know why.

11:35 AM Apr 29th from Tweetie

Hi, kids. On mend. (Thanks to tweet producer Lyn for filling in.) Hitting on Paki nurses in Spanglish. LOL. Old self!

12:33 PM Apr 29th from Tweetie

Medical query to Tweeps: Trying to remove drainage catheter from privates. Should I be wearing face mask?

12:49 PM Apr 29th from Tweetie

AAAAAAAAAAAAAAIIIIIIIIIIIIIIIIEEEEEEEEEEEEEEEEEEEEE EEEEEEEEEEEEEEE!!!!!!!!!!!!!!!!!

1:02 PM Apr 29th from Tweetie

Okay, got the catheter out. Thanks for help, everyone!

1:03 PM Apr 29th from Tweetie

Roland_Hedley

✔Following

BTW, effective today, Fox sez have 2 monetize feed. Shorter tweets. Sucks. [Paid Advt: HI, BILLY MAYS HERE FOR OXI CLEAN!]

12:52 PM Apr 30th from web

Because of Paki time diff, Obama's First 100 Days was yesterday. Please stop RTing blah-blah about so-over milestone. [ADVT: Always going? Flomax]

2:04 PM Apr 30th from web

Turning in. Miss bedtime reading to kids, except for "Goodnight Moon" to youngest. Every goddamn night for 12 years. [ADVT: Yr ad here]

10:15 PM Apr 30th from web

Anyone know how to get on Suggested Users list? Need to pump up follower count for Twitter sweeps. Will sleep w/ whoever.

8:19 AM May 1st from web

Kids want to see movie "Earth," so pre-screening DVD on laptop for liberal bias. Spoiler alert: Polar bear starves b/c of George Bush. [ADVT: ShamWow sells self!]

8:14 PM May 1st from TweetDeck

"WICKED MORNING BREATH TODAY. MAY GO WITH EXTRA MOUTHWASH."
BIP! BIP! BIP!
"I'VE BEEN THINKING: WHY DO WE EVEN **NEED** A COMMERCE SECRETARY? I MEAN, **WHAT** COMMERCE?"
BIP! BIP! BIP!
"EVER NOTICE HOW MESMERIZING A BLINKING CURSOR CAN BE? I HAVE."
BIP! BIP! BIP!
TWEETS FOR TWITS.
OHMIGOD! HE'S MAKING JIFFY POP!
GO TO SLEEP, GIRL.
GB Trudeau

Roland_Hedley

✔Following

Just checked out of hospital. Anyone recall what city I'm in? Probably know like back of hand, but parking lot unfamiliar.

10:19 AM May 2nd from TwitterGadget

Pakistanis still don't get existential threat. On local news, weather girl tracks advancing Taliban.

12:53 PM May 2nd from TwitterGadget

Currently at 33° 42' 0" N, 73° 10' 0" E. Anyone know a good deli near me?

12:55 PM May 2nd from TwitterGadget

Thanks, @Fake_Jesus!

12:56 PM May 2nd from TwitterGadget

Phony Phisher of Men knows from lox! LOL

12:57 PM May 2nd from TwitterGadget

Pakistan caving on Islamic law 1 hour north of capital = Washington allowing Catholics to set up Inquisition in Baltimore.

10:26 AM May 3rd from web

Scheduled Twintervu w/ Pak Prez Zardari. Can't think of anything to ask him, so may cancel. [ADVT: Now run by Italians! Chrysler]

10:27 AM May 3rd from web

Any questions, Tweeps? Nothing obvious, inane, or about you, please!
[ADVT: It's just that easy! Steam Buddy]

10:30 AM May 3rd from web

Pak Prez Zardari a no-show, apparently in London catching a few shows. Back on hotel room balcony, watching tracers.

11:09 AM May 3rd from twhirl

Pakistan crazy. Islamabad = 21st century. Swat Valley = 13th century. Bruner = 18th century with privileges. [ADVT: Not sold in stores! GM]

7:28 AM May 4th from web

Can't decide whether to go home for kid's ball game Friday or stay for the fall of Islamabad. Don't want to miss either.

9:13 AM May 4th from web

Always try to put family first. I can't say enough about what that says about me, especially with only 140 characters.

9:14 AM May 4th from web

THE TWEETS OF ROLAND HEDLEY, CONT'D.
"I REFUSE TO APOLOGIZE FOR MAKING TIME FOR MY KID'S BALL GAMES. SO I USUALLY END UP NOT GOING."

Spotted two heavily armed psycho-jihadists in lobby checking in for "convention." The complacency here is unbelievable.

9:05 AM May 5th from TweetDeck

No one looks up from newspaper as psycho-jihadists cane bellboy for whistling. Today's headline: "Growing Threat from India."

9:05 AM May 5th from TweetDeck

Having off the record heart-to-heart with one of the jihadists poolside. Is under a lot of pressure, admits he could really go for a margarita.

2:18 PM May 5th from TweetDeck

Producer Lyn looking better every day, but affair could get back to mistress, already holding more cards than I'm comfortable with.

10:35 AM May 6th from RSS2Twitter

John Edwards mess real wake-up call. Crunched the numbers and don't think I can afford both Hamptons rental and hush money.

10:36 AM May 6th from RSS2Twitter

Islamabad update: Jihadist "guests" set fire to hotel bar while journos try to watch Celtics game. Indian businessman detained as suspect.

10:45 AM May 7th from web

Only other bar in hotel trashed week ago by Sri Lankan soccer hooligans. Indian housekeeper detained as suspect.

10:46 AM May 7th from web

Swat refugees stream into hotel. Manager distraught, claims refugees not green, won't re-use towels or bathwater.

10:50 AM May 7th from web

Hapless jihadists get lost, accidentally wander into ballroom packed w/ 600 refugees. Over quickly.

11:09 AM May 7th from web

Roland_Hedley

✔Following

Pakistani leaders seek $1 billion aid to save country, but indignant over US request not to steal it. Deserve upcoming fate.

1:18 PM May 7th from web

1.4 mil-man Pak Army still can't defeat rag-tag foe that has no tanks, artillery, air support. Indian Army reaction: "Interesting."

11:17 AM May 8th from web

Ordered home to cover Ashton Kutner, guest @ WH Correspondents dinner. Paradox: Leaving war zone but want to kill myself.

12:22 PM May 8th from Winbox

Lyn here. RH 2 cover Ashton K @ WH din. Way awkward b/c of vast follower count disparity. Pls tweet encouragement. Our secret.

12:54 PM May 8th from TwitterBerry

Flight delayed. Anyone have 411 on Ashby Kutler? Not on Google. Assuming holds some record for amount of spare time.

1:01 PM May 8th from Winbox

Met @ Dulles by Lyn for briefer on Ashton Cupcake coverage @ WH journo din tonight. Acquired sked, coordinates.

2:45 PM May 9th from TwitterBerry

---

411 on Kutcher: As a person, models, pitches, punks, tweets, and, presumably, honks. As an actor, stretches, grows.

2:48 PM May 9th from TwitterBerry

Latest Cupcake coordinates 38°54’38”N 77°03’05”W; Lyn has eyes on. I know this b/c she’s hyperventilating into my IFB.

4:47 PM May 9th from web

Arr. Hilton, photogs yell name. I pivot, flash guns, baby blues. Turns out blocking shot of some TV teen star enjoying minute 3 of 15.

6:09 PM May 9th from txt

Cupcake arrives Hilton. Pandemonium. Like Beatlemania, only unreasoning. In cynical bid for “aw” from media, Ashton w/ Mom.

6:29 PM May 9th from web

Correction. Not Mom. [ADVT: Better than sex. As if. Star Trek]

6:30 PM May 9th from web

Roland_Hedley

✓Following

Michael Steele schmoozing Cupcake, sez he tweets too, that RNC has over 700 followers, woot, woot! Ashton pats him on head.

7:14 PM May 9th from web

Still @ pre-party hosted by bankrupt L.A. Times for losers w/o din invites. Any Tweep @ dinner who has Cupcake in sightline?

8:00 PM May 9th from web

Ashton tells table Twitter more "paradigm-shifting" invention than telephone. Wife takes away his cell. Caves in 5 min.

8:19 PM May 9th from web

POTUS must be speaking. Laughter too loud, smug, socialist. Accident only balanced journotwit not @ prom? You decide.

9:21 PM May 9th from web

OK, I understand standing O for Obama from journolibs, waiters. But from Secret Service? Hate it when heavy drinking is politicized.

9:36 PM May 9th from web

Breaking. By jumping up and down, can just see top of Tom Cruise's head.

9:42 PM May 9th from web

Val Kilmer just came out, puked on my shoes, returned. Will make some state a fine senator.

9:58 PM May 9th from web

In last 3 hours, Ashton Kutcher parties, adds 34,516 followers. Sober, I lose 9. Need more proof no God? Going home.

11:09 PM May 9th from Winbox

Roland_Hedley

✓ Following

Minutes away: Trump to rule on moral fitness of semi-nude ditz to stay in cheesy contest. Could cut suspense w/ chainsaw.

9:58 AM May 12th from web

At issue: Moral difference between semi-nude posing for sleazy photographer and semi-nude posing for tacky judges.

10:06 AM May 12th from web

Breaking. Steamed Trump delays presser because of "lame" NTSB hearing on Buffalo plane crash. Suspense building.

10:12 AM May 12th from web

Prejean pre-positioned. Trump arrives.

10:13 AM May 12th from web

Oh, whatever will be her fate?

10:14 AM May 12th from web

He's "reviewed the pictures very carefully"! Done his homework!

10:14 AM May 12th from web

Pictures are "fine"! (On account of this being the 21st century.) YAAAAAAAAAY!

10:15 AM May 12th from web

Has made "determination." "Carrie will remain Miss California!" A great, great, awesome, humongous, wise, awesome determination!

10:16 AM May 12th from web

Uh-oh. Asking Carrie to say a "few words."

10:17 AM May 12th from web

Carrie thanks us for thousands of letters of support, although too many to count.

10:18 AM May 12th from web

Grandfather served at Battle of Bulge. Taught her never to back down.

10:22 AM May 12th from web

Roland_Hedley

✔Following

OMG, photos #3, #4, #7 were Photoshopped! So wrong about this conference not making news. Apologies.
10:25 AM May 12th from web

Breaking: Carrie will stay true to who she is.
10:34 AM May 12th from web

Carrie explaining. "Photographer got some sort of shot of me while I was exposed."
10:37 AM May 12th from web

"It's like a photographer getting a picture of you getting dressed. I've learned from that."
10:38 AM May 12th from web

Trump: "If Carrie were an average man, this would not be an issue." Really good point.
10:39 AM May 12th from web

BEST. PRESSER. EVER.
10:44 AM May 12th from web

OH, GOD... IT'S 7:20 ALREADY. TIME FOR MY NEXT TWEET!
I GOT NOTHIN'! NOTHIN'!
YOU'RE LATE!
WHERE R U?
WHAT'S WRONG?
BING! BING! BING!
"GUESS WHO JUST MET ME IN MY HOTEL SUITE. HOUSE-HOLD NAME."
BEYONCÉ!
HILLARY!
OPRAH!
TAP! TAP! TAP!
A DESPER-ATE MAN.
IT'S MY FOLLOWERS! THEY'RE **IN-SATIABLE!**
ROSIE!
ENYA!
DICK CHENEY!
GB Trudeau

Roland_Hedley

▸ ✓Following

Had to go see kids' school psychologist. On Career Day, my oldest allegedly told class he wanted to be a "sex worker."

12:40 PM May 14th from RSS2Twitter

Brought along Cody's personal therapist, who called out school shrink for intervention, stepping on kid's dream.

12:41 PM May 14th from RSS2Twitter

Compromise: Cody to put "hospitality industry" on his Career Day poster.

12:41 PM May 14th from RSS2Twitter

As part of settlement, have just agreed to give speech today to class about careers on Twitter. Anyone know of one?

12:42 PM May 14th from RSS2Twitter

Great. Per your replies, only ones monetizing Twitter are sex workers.

12:48 PM May 14th from the RSS2Twitter

Sources: If John Boehner joined on Hill by tanning protégé Charlie Crist, skin cancer poster boy John McCain to push back.

1:14 PM May 14th from web

Point of Boehner tan: To look good. Effect of Boehner tan: To be widely mocked. Does the man even HAVE a staff?

1:15 PM May 14th from web

Point of Charlie Crist tan: To promote Sunshine State. Reaction to Charlie Crist tan: They have tanning salons in Florida?

3:42 PM May 14th from web

Picking up rumor re: Charlie Crist that I refuse to repeat. Important that legit journos set good example for bloggers.

4:33 PM May 14th from web

Per Fox: 1. Torture's legal, saved lives. 2. Pelosi evil for supporting. Note: Do NOT try to make both points @ same time.

1:14 PM May 15th from web

Celebrated 300th tweet last night w/ buds. You wouldn't believe what Biden said in his toast, so no point in repeating it.

8:42 AM May 16th from TwitterBerry

Shoeshine guy, who has some unpronounceable Slavic name, always keeps it real, even without a tip. Feel grounded for the day.

10:15 AM May 16th from TweetDeck

I'm black and blue from all your nudges. Sorry the feed was down yesterday. Needed another me day.

7:22 AM May 18th from web

On deck: exclusive twinterview with my field manicurist. Check out how the pros keep their thumbs groomed on the road.

10:39 AM May 18th from web

NYT's Krugman makes Newsweek cover b/c his "views seem more than a little plausible." Bar so low my bookie could clear it.

9:27 AM Mar 29th from web

Why do journotwits ask for questions? Do pilots ask passengers how to land? Do surgeons ask patients where to cut? Do your job, brah!

11:18 AM Mar 23rd from TwitterGadget

Just had morning joe out in the garden listening to "real" tweets. No added value at all. Nature so overrated.

7:17 AM Mar 24th from TwitterGadget

Suggested POTUS Notre Dame commencement open: "Graduates, Faculty, Parents, Friends, Unborn Innocents . . ." Could work.

1:04 PM May 17th from web

Why are unborn always described as innocent? What difference would it make if they were guilty of something? Still people.

1:22 PM May 17th from web

That rumor about Charlie Crist is now completely out of control. It's nobody's business, so do NOT retweet this.

8:47 AM May 18th from txt

SKULL & BONES, GEORGE W. BUSH'S YALE SECRET SOCIETY, IS BACK IN THE NEWS. ROLAND HEDLEY HAS MORE.
INDEED I DO, BRET, WHICH WILL COME AS NO SURPRISE TO READERS OF MY BLOG, "ROLLIN' WITH ROLAND," OR TO MY FOLLOWERS ON TWITTER ...
FOX
... MY FRIENDS ON FACEBOOK OR MY FAN BASE AT MYSPACE! A BIG SHOUT-OUT TO ALL OF YOU! BRET?
FOX news
UM ... WHAT ABOUT THE STORY, ROLAND?
WHOA! THIS JUST IN, BRET – I'M BEING CALLED OUT FOR MY SHOUT-OUT!

Roland_Hedley

✓Following

In New Haven on some sort of big story. Meeting local followers at Starbucks. Line around the block.

11:46 AM Mar 9th from Tweetie

Taking coffee out to some of the followers waiting in the cold to see me. Amazed expressions. People don't expect that from a celebrity.

11:50 AM Mar 9th from Tweetie

Waiting to do standup in front of Yale's Battell Chapel. Think I'll duck in to thank God personally for cable. Be right back.

2:15 PM Mar 9th from Tweetie

Wow. Ever studied the 10 Commandments? Only 6 are about us. The first 4 are all about protecting the Big Guy's brand. Talk about narcissism.

2:34 PM Mar 9th from Tweetie

Can't find url for Bible. You'll have to trust me on this.

2:40 PM Mar 9th from Tweetie

Roland_Hedley

✔ Following

Did "Whither News?" panel at Yale last night. Argued tweet-driven news is future. You decide, we report. Standing O.

9:51 AM Mar 12th from web

While speaking last night, someone threw panties on stage. Or boxers. Whatever. Times like that, always ask myself, "What would The Boss do?"

10:13 PM Mar 12th from web

Any of you recall when I first began my journey on Twitter? Try to remember, and if you remember, then follow, follow, follow.

3:32 PM Mar 17th from UberTwitter

Poll: Baby Boomers say old age begins at 80, three years more than US life expectancy. Death is the new Old.

1:15 PM May 19th from web

Before I open my eyes in a.m., I like to guess where I am. I usually get it wrong, but it's a little game I like to play.

8:11 AM May 21st from web

Blessings, Minister of Diamonds dies, leaving you $30 mil. Send bank info asap. Ha! Would never, ever fall for that again.

8:27 AM May 22nd from web

DID PRESCOTT BUSH PINCH THE SKULL OF GERONIMO, AS HE ALLEGEDLY CLAIMED?
AND WHAT KIND OF STUDENT "SOCIETY" LOOTS GRAVES, ANYWAY? ROLAND HEDLEY HAS MORE.
UH ... ROLAND? HEAR ME? ROLAND?
GB Trudeau
"ABOUT TO INTERVIEW MYSELF. SEND QUESTIONS."
ROLAND!
TAP! TAP! TAP!
GB Trudeau

Roland_Hedley

✔Following

This is Lyn. Trying to get Roland to provide live tweetage of GOP Chair Steele speech. Stand by.

12:29 PM May 19th from twhirl

He's eating lunch and can't be bothered. Could someone direct message him, please? Oh, never mind, here he comes . . .

12:31 PM May 19th from twhirl

Okay, I'm back live. Turning on the damn speech so you don't have to.

12:32 PM May 19th from web

"Era of GOP apologizing for past over." Feel like an idiot, didn't know it'd started. You'd think I'd notice an entire era.

12:36 PM May 19th from web

So far, Steele has used zero dated hip-hop slang. No longer reaching out to ballers. Tent shrinking . . .

12:38 PM May 19th from web

GOP chickens out on vote to rebrand Dems as "Democrat Socialist Party." Fox up all night changing graphics.

11:33 AM May 20th from web

"Democrat Socialist" not scary enough anyway. GOP should try "National Socialist." Sounds similar, but makes them Nazis.

11:35 AM May 20th from web

3000 dead 9/11 = 2 unending wars. 120,000 gun deaths since 9/11 = looser gun laws. A Martian wouldn't fathom, but fuck him.

1:25 PM May 20th from web

Anyone know where the president is right now? Never mind, I'll call his private cell, it'd be faster.

10:51 AM May 22nd from RSS2Twitter

Breaking: Ashton Kutcher promises to leave Twitter. Good on him for sparing 2 million tweeps hourly brain farts.

11:18 PM May 26th from web

Correction: Editor says Kutcher "threatened" to stop tweeting, not "promised." Who cares as long as he stops?

11:20 PM May 26th from web

Roland_Hedley

✔Following

CA court to gays: In your face. Yes! Like Newt, believe marriage is between man and woman and another woman and another woman.

11:34 AM May 27th from Twitterrific

Pity guy who updates Roland Burris cemetery monument. What to add? "Pay to Player"? Tough call when etched in stone.

10:04 AM May 28th from web

Brushing up on hieroglyphics for POTUS Egypt trip. Anyone know how two reeds, a moon, and an owl is pronounced?

10:08 AM May 28th from web

Time for North Korea regime change. Easy to vaporize leaders, who all live in manse cluster. Wouldn't even disturb neighbors.

10:25 AM May 28th from web

Fun hearing GOP call Sotomayor "racist." For 200 years, conservatives thought it was a compliment. Party's grown.

1:10 PM May 28th from UberTwitter

"GAY INROADS ASIDE, STILL BELIEVE MARRIAGE IS SACRED INSTITUTION. EVEN MY SECOND MARRIAGE WAS HOLY HELL."

Oppose Sotomayor but understand pride in Hispanic Thurgood Marshall, like when Rick Sanchez became Cuban Ted Baxter. I get it.

2:19 PM May 28th from UberTwitter

Gotta respect Susan Boyle. Not only overcame two of the cheesiest songs ever written, but swears like Cheney.

8:41 AM May 29th from UberTwitter

I get her swears; fame can be toxic. Lost pals in junior high when I changed my name after star turn in "Oklahoma!"

8:45 AM May 29th from UberTwitter

Roland_Hedley

✓Following

Twittering about Binging vs. Googling and then FedExing replies home to Xerox on Kleenex while enjoying Coke from a Thermos.

1:30 PM May 29th from UberTwitter

At gym, watching CNN's Sanchez "get it" w/ tweets, posts, calls, polls, honks. Viewers as news. New paradigm? Will Bing.

2:14 PM May 29th from txt

Still @ gym. MSNBC reporting Senate to question Sonya on her "bench demeanor," aka judging while Hispanic. Fruit on head? Legit concern.

2:42 PM May 29th from txt

Speaking of bench demeanor, bold-faced name pressing weights next to me tooting with every lift.

2:44 PM May 29th from txt

In steam room. Bold-faced name followed me in. Not cool to stalk fellow bold-faced name. Ringing for attendant.

2:49 PM May 29th from txt

Twitter divided between Suggested Users, who get money for nothin', chicks for free, and rest of us. Living in two Americas.

8:41 PM May 30th from web

Have relearned Hieroglyphic for POTUS Egypt trip. If curse of mummy kicks in, will be one of few who can reason with undead.

10:32 AM Jun 1st from web

Moses must have spoken Hieroglyphic as well as Jewish, or he never could've talked Pharaoh out of entire labor force.

10:34 AM Jun 1st from web

Not sure relationship w/ Chloe can survive Egypt trip. The story is my mistress now, and she's a jealous mistress indeed!

10:36 AM Jun 1st from web

Thinking of breaking up w/ her anyway to reset marriage. Per Wall St., hard to game system w/o sound fundamentals @ home.

10:38 AM Jun 1st from web

Sorry, realize comparing marriage to economic downturn sounds cold. Cue stimulus package jokes to lighten mood!

10:40 AM Jun 1st from web

Roland_Hedley

✓Following

Riyadh. Having flashback to first visit as underbriefed cub reporter, wore veil to interview King Abdullah. Live and learn!

4:20 PM Jun 3rd from TwitterGadget

Economic downturn even affecting Kingdom. Roadside littered w/ abandoned Mercedes. Collecting hood ornaments for my kids.

4:26 PM Jun 3rd from TwitterGadget

POTUS hugs/kisses king, saves bows/grovels for speech to Arab “street.” Wearing my “Apology Tour ’09” satin crew jacket.

7:03 PM Jun 3rd from TwitterGadget

With Arab “street” placated, Apology Tour ’09 rolls into Dresden, where POTUS to apologize for winning World War II.

6:48 PM Jun 4th from web

Report: After expressing regret for trashing Normandy on D-Day, POTUS to formally apologize to French for Lance Armstrong.

11:46 PM Jun 4th from web

Germans take POTUS on "What were we thinking?" tour of Buchenwald, while I pre-position in Paris for Excusez-Moi Day.

1:32 PM Jun 5th from web

Meal tweet: Un verre de Chardonnay, deux pains au chocolat, un peu de foie gras, et un plat des Freedom Fries.

1:40 PM Jun 5th from web

If, dans le jour ahead, vous feel j'ai tweeté something offensif, permittez-moi to say en avance: Je suis désolé.

2:19 PM Jun 5th from web

Sorry to go all Continental on you. Didn't get to speak Hieroglyphic in Egypt, and needed to feed my language jones!

2:30 PM Jun 5th from web

Met @ Dulles by Chloe, who's aging in reverse. More beautiful now than when we met in April. Fingers crossed for July.

12:36 PM Jun 8th from TweetDeck

...AND HE TWEETED DURING THE **ENTIRE** BROADCAST! CAN YOU PLEASE EXPLAIN THE TWITTER APPEAL TO ME?
IT'S JUST A SIMPLE OVERSHARING TOOL, MIKE. IT'S LIKE A FRISBEE — HARMLESS INTERACTIVE FUN!
IT HAS ITS PRACTICAL USES. BUT I PREDICT MOST PEOPLE WILL COME TO REALIZE IT'S A BANAL TIME-SUCK AND MOVE ON. UNTIL THEN, ENJOY!
"UPSIDE TO GOING GRAY: NOSE HAIRS NO LONGER VISIBLE ON CAMERA."

Roland_Hedley

✔Following

More cuts @ Fox, shutting down 9 tweet feeds. These are real people w/ families, all of them fair + balanced. Tragique.

12:45 PM Jun 8th from RSS2Twitter

To put human face on Fox cuts, fired DC tweet bureau chief fought to keep MY feed up. Frank somebody. Well done, Frank!

3:22 PM Jun 8th from RSS2Twitter

Karl Rove accepts gigs online, so booked him for son's 9th birthday. Kids taunted him for being soft, fat, pink. Cruel age.

7:34 PM Jun 9th from web

Rove never learned to drive, so I took him home. Seemed wistful about Dubya, called their relationship "bromance with wars."

7:45 PM Jun 9th from web

KR sad case. Fell for Bush swagger, made him prez, thanked w/ "Turd Blossom." Deserves better. Son suggests "Miss Piggy."

8:14 PM Jun 9th from web

Roland_Hedley

✔ Following

Just had drink w/ fired Fox tweeters. Notice they all talk in short, choppy bursts, sound impaired. Hello, Workers' Comp!

8:23 PM Jun 9th from web

Going into tanning booth, so will be off-feed for 20 mins. Replies fielded by tweet producer Lyn, so keep 'em clean, gang!

11:06 AM Jun 10th from txt

Lyn here. My name is actually spelled Lynn, but RH doesn't like to "waste" extra character. So classy.

11:07 AM Jun 10th from TweetDeck

Bumped into John Boehner, irritating b/c requested private booth. Still, props: even toes color of fine Corinthian leather.

11:54 AM Jun 10th from txt

Letterman: Palin updates "slutty" stew look at Bloomie's. Palin retort: Never went to Bloomie's. Needs outrage advisor.

6:08 AM Jun 11th from web

Wish we had color-coded voters like Iran. If we all wore red or blue, exit polls a snap. Downside: Pushback from gangs.

11:57 AM Jun 12th from RSS2Twitter

GHWB birthday skydiving alert. Has it been 5 years already? In role reversal, 43 watches 41 in freefall.

12:38 PM Jun 12th from web

Jews won't let Wright talk to POTUS? Get over yourself, dude. They won't let ME talk to him, either, don't see me crying.

1:46 PM Jun 12th from web

Updates fly by. To follow many is to follow nobody. Matrix of meaninglessness. Cool idea for a tweet. Hope you enjoyed it.

7:50 PM Jun 14th from web

To give updates meaning, unfollow everyone but besties like me. Serious. If you're not reading this, you're proving my point.

8:16 PM Jun 14th from web

Lyn here. Rollie just crashed. Sorry about the unified theory of tweeting. Please don't unfollow. I'll get blamed.

8:24 PM Jun 14th from web

Roland_Hedley

Following

Twitter proving itself today in Tehran. Leading Mousavi supporter in Saadatabad district just tweeted dinner plans.

12:39 PM Jun 15th from web

Tehran RT @FakeMousavi. Trapped by Basij between Andarzgu and Dowlat St. Need to attract 200,000 followers asap. Tips?

1:10 PM Jun 15th from web

Followers: Let's all stay off Twitter today so updates don't bump brave, moving tweets from Iranian freedom-fighters.

9:42 AM Jun 16th from Twitterrific

Okay, okay, back off. It was just a suggestion. Bad idea. Sheesh.

9:43 AM Jun 16th from Twitterrific

The Revolution will be tweeted. Cynics: Show me the business model. Me: Done. [ADVT: Stand w/ Free Iran. Mousavi for Prez]

8:19 AM Jun 17th from web

"NIGHT STILL FILLED WITH HAUNTING CRIES OF ALLAHU AKBAR SHOUTED FROM ROOF-TOPS..."
"BASIJ THUGS GOING DOOR-TO-DOOR. DAN-GER EVERY-WHERE."
WOW...
"@ ROLAND HEDLEY: YR REPORTS R AWESOME. RU REALLY TWEETING FROM IRAN?"
CLIK!
CLIK!
CLIKITY!
©B Trudeau
"@ SAM: RETWEETING. SIMILAR."
BIP!
BIP!

Roland_Hedley

✓Following

Though she hearts Iranian revolution, wife won't use green avatar overlay b/c makes her look "slimy." Any way to correct?

3:44 PM Jun 17th from txt

Still watching noisy young marchers in green brawling in streets. Allahu Akbar = Erin Go Braugh. Miss New York.

10:16 AM Jun 18th from web

Economy claims another victim. Nevada Sen. John Ensign busts self over year-old affair because can't afford blackmail.

11:00 AM Jun 18th from web

In line w/ cool kids outside Apple store waiting for midnight release of 3Gs iPhone. Mood giddy. People dressed as apps.

7:17 PM Jun 18th from web

Apple Store line abuzz w/ news that Ken Starr endorses Sotomayor. Big deal, as this means sex life thoroughly vetted.

7:52 PM Jun 18th from web

RTing this to my queuemates outside Apple Store: @adamisacson "CNN: Reading Twitter To Old People Since 2009." LOL

9:23 PM Jun 18th from TwitterBerry

---

4 mins until Apple opens doors for 3Gs launch! Pale young men in line excitedly discussing first thing they'll cut and paste.

11:56 PM Jun 18th from TwitterBerry

Rumor sweeps through crowd of a Ryan Seacrest app for new iPhone, although no one has clue what it does.

11:59 PM Jun 18th from TwitterBerry

Doors open, then close to control crowd. Geniuses w/ wireless card swipers move in, suck disposable income from room.

12:01 AM Jun 19th from TwitterBerry

Finally made it home w/ 3Gs. Early takeaway? New iPhone off the hook. Damn thing's in the next room making me a Panini.

10:37 AM Jun 19th from TwitterBerry

Leaving for black-tie Radio/TV journo dinner to show off 3Gs. New app called iHero tells me I look great.

5:35 PM Jun 19th from TwitterBerry

Roland_Hedley

✔Following

Governor Sanford kicks off 2012 campaign by disappearing, paradoxically raising national profile. Crazy like Fox.

2:07 PM Jun 22nd from twhirl

Report: Sanford wandering in wilderness, triggering excited speculation from GOP faithful that he'll return with tablets.

9:03 PM Jun 22nd from TwitterFox

Stimulus package spending out of control: Appalachian Trail extended to Argentina.

10:29 AM Jun 24th from web

Sanford story checking out. Campers in Ecuador, Bolivia, Paraguay report sightings of fast-moving, naked hiker.

10:48 AM Jun 24th from web

Prearranged for me to ask second question at Sanford presser. Will be reading question from Argentinean hiker.

11:02 AM Jun 24th from TwitterFox

Sanford apologizes for 7 minutes. Won't say for what.

12:09 PM Jun 24th from TwitterFox

Holy crap.

12:11 PM Jun 24th from TwitterFox

Just terminated 14 innocent email relationships. No more direct messages, please.

12:12 PM Jun 24th from TwitterFox

Roland_Hedley

✓**Following**

Stand by for three-part tweet. Please RT to followers so they can stand by as well.

10:42 AM Jun 26th from web

Travails of Sanford, Ensign et al remind me of line from Michael Caine movie "Alfie," a line I've always tried to live by.

10:43 AM Jun 26th from web

"When I look back on all the birds I've known, all they've done for me, the little I've done for them, I ask meself, what's it all about?"

10:44 AM Jun 26th from web

So what do you think, tweeps? What's it all about? Best answer will be retweeted to secret list of 4 million followers.

10:44 AM Jun 26th from web

By the way, "It is what it is" is not an answer to "What's it all about?"

10:45 AM Jun 26th from web

1:15 p.m. Boys come down for breakfast, join National Conversation on Fatherhood with usual chorus of "You suck, Dad."

1:16 PM Jun 21st from web

Lame Father's Day, or as my kids hilariously call it, Supreme Leader Day.

2:55 PM Jun 21st from web

Someone just tweeted "Perez Hilton Assaulted by Will.i.am." Paris Hilton's sister assaulted by a bunch of typos? WTF?

8:57 AM Jun 22nd from web

Fun fact: Of the many women with whom I've crossed the line, all but one currently have green icons.

9:26 PM Jun 25th from web

Wife to announce results of family debt load audit 6 p.m. EDT. Fear scrutiny of stakeholders like Victoria's Secret.

9:21 AM Jun 27th from Winbox

Yes! Wife releases details of family finance stress test, Victoria's Secret not on Amex bill! Up on roof shouting Allahu Akbar.

11:53 AM Jun 27th from Winbox

Roland_Hedley

✓Following

Stonewall event at WH. SO many great gay jokes POTUS could've told yesterday if yesterday had been 1969 and not 40th anniversary of 1969.

10:48 AM Jun 30th from RSS2Twitter

Obama to host July 4 BBQ for military families w/ jumbotron to watch intercept of North Korean rocket. Good luck, Hawaii!

2:45 PM Jul 2nd from web

US admits 10% chance of missile shield failure. Under Obama, military can-do downgraded to might-do.

3:17 PM Jul 2nd from web

Joe Plumber calls for Chris Dodd to be lynched. Don't approve, but so great he hasn't faded away, still wants to contribute.

9:28 AM Jul 3rd from TweetDeck

Thanks to HiDef, unexpected renegotiation of contract. Sticking point seems to be a few lousy broken nose capillaries.

1:57 PM Jul 3rd from web

ROLAND? A WORD?
HOLD ON, I'M MID-TWEET...
"BOSS WANTS 2 TALK. WONDER WHAT IT'S ABOUT. THOUGHTS?"
"PROBABLY WANTS 2 DISCUSS MY SIZZLING DEBUT IN HI-DEF."
CLIK! CLIK! CLIK!
©B Trudeau
WE NEED TO DISCUSS YOUR DE-BUT IN HD.
"BINGO. ASK 4 RAISE?"
CLIK! CLIK! CLIK!

Roland_Hedley

✓ Following

Palin gives incoherent 2,606-word speech in 14:20, or 192 wpm. I've said this before, folks: meth. People laughed. Now?

7:33 PM Jul 3rd from Twitterrific

Doubt Vanity Fair piece on Palin was last straw, as was fair, balanced, in places. In fact, still haunted by 2 words: "Indisputably fertile."

7:35 PM Jul 3rd from Twitterrific

BTW, Palin's 2606-word speech = 14,888 characters. Had she resigned on Twitter, it would have taken 106.3 tweets.

7:52 PM July 3rd from Twitterrific

POTUS meets w/ diminutive Russian "counterpart" Dmitry Medvedev today. Like meeting Mickey instead of Walt Disney.

9:54 AM Jul 6th from web

Obama looks into eyes of Medvedev, sees soul in full flight wearing nothing but Aeroflot hand towel.

10:14 AM Jul 6th from web

Grief-stricken Joe Jackson stoically appears before press w/ MJ brand manager Al Sharpton to launch new record label.

11:49 AM Jun 29th from web

Per Joe Jackson, MJ's children "happy" because surrounded by kids "their own size."

11:51 AM Jun 29th from web

MJ's legacy is . . . hold it! There's a police chase on I-635 in Dallas! Excellent, presser was a downer. Thank you, MSNBC!

11:55 AM Jun 29th from web

Breaking: Al Sharpton to join Dallas police chase perp at press conference tomorrow a.m., pending his survival.

12:12 PM Jun 29th from web

MSNBC interrupts exciting police chase w/ sound bites from MJ presser, which is so over. Let it go, guys.

12:19 PM Jun 29th from web

Roland_Hedley

Following

Covered live by nets, massive bereaved fan base says ciao to beloved pedophile. Only in America and 167 other countries.

10:09 AM Jul 7th from web

Bereaved millions stay home to ogle open coffin of beloved pedophile on live TV. Earth about to get a little bit creepier.

10:25 AM Jul 7th from web

12-yr-old talent finalist chosen by family to impersonate beloved pedophile at memorial. Jackson 4 officially tone-deaf.

10:34 AM Jul 7th from web

Moscow: POTUS irked by MJ questions, hopes “focus” will soon return to nuke arms. Can’t wait to cover, as sky will be thick w/ pigs.

11:50 AM Jul 7th from web

People lining LA overpasses to watch MJ driven down freeway with massive police escort. Like OJ, only at 15 mph.

12:34 PM Jul 7th from web

"Service" begins. Millions who are being paid to work are actually watching TV. Loss in global productivity today = GNP of Mexico.

1:10 PM Jul 7th from web

Audio probs. While we wait, let's discuss probability that MJ coffin will be wheeled out to, uh, cheers. Could be awkward.

1:27 PM July 7th from web

Mariah Carey appears at service displaying tribute cleavage.

1:45 PM Jul 7th from web

Roland_Hedley

✔Following

Brooke Shields compares 50-year-old black entertainer to The Little Prince, a tiny towhead who lives on Asteroid B612.

2:00 PM Jul 7th from web

12-year-old Brit MJ impersonator sticks it, whisked out side door, flown directly to his new life in Vegas.

2:23 PM Jul 7th from web

Close call here. They ended “We Are the World” before I could jimmy open my gun closet and blow my brains out.

2:33 PM Jul 7th from web

Sorry, folks, after all free MJ coverage, gotta pay some bills. [ADVT: Building court-approved models since early June. GM]

9:51 AM Jul 8th from web

[ADVT: Information doesn’t really want to be free. It wants to be bound, gagged, forced through eye of needle. Fox News]

9:51 AM Jul 8th from web

RIP Bob McNamara, star of "Best, Brightest," whose widely influential title signaled birth of irony. Stopped many doors.

9:20 AM Jul 6th from TwitterGadget

First saw McNamara @ Pentagon presser explaining VC body count algorithms. During demo, mainframe kept rounding up! Hilarious.

9:39 AM Jul 6th from TwitterGadget

Okay, this is just a coincidence, but my housekeeper begins a lot of sentences with "As a wise Latina once told me . . ."

12:58 PM July 13th from web

At Sotomayor hearing, GOP Message of the Day: "We don't want a single Hispanic vote. Ever. Done. Tent flap down. Over." Interesting direction.

1:06 PM Jul 13th from web

Häs änyönë ëlsë's Twïttër äccöünt bëën ïnfëctëd by Brünö büg? Nöt fünny.

9:57 AM Jul 15th from web

Gréât. Brünó büg júst mûtätéd.

10:17 AM Jul 15th from web

Roland_Hedley

✓ Following

The night Donna P. let me into her pants, Armstrong walked on moon. So never saw it, but will always remember where I was.

3:37 PM Jul 20th from web

We broke up shortly thereafter, so did get to see Buzz Aldrin.

3:38 PM Jul 20th from web

To "fill void," wife decides to accept Gitmo detainee. Hoping to get one who's not falsely accused, as less bitter.

11:37 PM Jul 20th from web

Agree in principle concealed guns should give criminals second thoughts. Hitch: Most criminals don't have first thoughts.

3:05 PM Jul 22nd from twhirl

New pal @AKGovSarahPalin seeks tweet editor. Can't be tight-ass about syntax, grammar, meaning, facts, sense. Reply direct.

4:18 PM Jul 22nd from twhirl

The time you spend reading this tweet is gone, lost forever, carrying you closer to death. Am trying not to abuse privilege.

10:24 AM Jul 23rd from web
